smoothies and juices

simple and delicious easy-to-make recipes

Christine Ambridge

This is a Parragon Publishing Book
First published in 2002

Parragon Publishing
Queen Street House
4 Queen Street
Bath BA1 1HE, UK

Copyright © Parragon 2002

ISBN: 0-75259-675-6

Printed in China

Produced by the Bridgewater Book Company Ltd.

Photographer Calvey Taylor-Haw

Home Economist Michaela Haw

NOTES FOR THE READER

• This book uses both metric and imperial
measurements. Follow the same units of
measurement throughout; do not mix metric
and imperial.

• All spoon measurements are level: teaspoons
are assumed to be 5 ml, and tablespoons are
assumed to be 15 ml.

• Unless otherwise stated, milk is assumed to
be whole milk, eggs and individual vegetables
such as carrots are medium, and pepper is
freshly ground black pepper.

• Recipes using raw eggs should be avoided
by infants, the elderly, pregnant women,
convalescents, and anyone suffering from
an illness.

• The times given are an approximate guide
only. Preparation times differ according to
the techniques used by different people and
the cooking times may also vary from those
given. Optional ingredients, variations, or
serving suggestions have not been included
in the calculations.

contents

introduction

There has never been a better time to enjoy the wonderful benefits of smoothies and juices. Our local stores and supermarkets are bursting with tantalizing fresh fruits and vegetables, and many of them are in plentiful supply all year round.

You can also enjoy seasonal fruits at any time of year simply by freezing them. Peel them first if necessary, cut into slices or cubes, then arrange them in a single layer on a tray and freeze them. You can then transfer them to freezer bags, ready for use.

The drinks in this book are quick to prepare, easy to digest, and full of vitamins, minerals, and other life-enhancing substances. Bananas, for example, are a rich source of potassium and magnesium, and can help lower cholesterol levels. Mangoes are full of vitamin A, which is a powerful cancer-fighting agent. Pineapples contain bromelain, an enzyme that helps ease inflammation and soothes the digestion; and tomatoes contain vitamin E, a valuable antioxidant that helps combat the aging process.

You can enjoy the drinks in this book at any time of day. Within these pages you will find refreshing morning pick-me-ups, nutritious lunchtime drinks, delicious dinner combinations, and stunning concoctions for entertaining that will have your guests coming back for more. So, whatever the time of day, or whatever the occasion, this book will ensure you have the perfect drink every time.

cinnamon & lemon tea

page 24

watercress float

page 42

pineapple soda

page 70

cherry kiss

page 92

morning refreshers

What better way to wake up than to treat your taste buds to an explosion of mouthwatering flavors? The delicious drinks in this section will uplift your senses and leave you feeling refreshed and ready for whatever the day will bring. Whether your idea of a good breakfast treat is an energizing Red Bell Pepper Booster, a cool Peppermint Ice, or a relaxing and luxurious Pacific Smoothie, there is bound to be something here to tempt you and ensure a perfect start to your day.

melon
medley

how hard ☀ extremely easy
serves ☀ two
prep time ☀ 15 minutes
cooking time ☀ —

ingredients

1 cup
plain yogurt

3½ oz/100 g
galia melon,
cut into chunks

3½ oz/100 g
cantaloupe melon,
cut into chunks

3½ oz/100 g
watermelon,
cut into chunks

6 ice cubes

to decorate
wedges of **melon**

☀ Pour the yogurt into a food processor. Add the galia melon chunks and process until smooth.

☀ Add the cantaloupe and watermelon chunks along with the ice cubes and process until smooth. Pour the mixture into glasses and decorate with wedges of melon. Serve at once.

fruit
cooler

how hard ✳ extremely easy

serves ✳ two

prep time ✳ 10 minutes

cooking time ✳ —

ingredients

1 cup
orange juice

½ cup
plain yogurt

2 eggs

2 bananas,
sliced and frozen

to decorate

slices of fresh
banana

✳ Pour the orange juice and yogurt into a food processor and process gently until combined.

✳ Add the eggs and frozen bananas and process until smooth. Pour the mixture into glasses and decorate the rims with slices of fresh banana. Add straws and serve.

pacific
smoothie

how hard ✳ extremely easy

serves ✳ two

prep time ✳ 15 minutes

cooking time ✳ 15 minutes

ingredients

1½ cups
hazelnut yogurt

2 tbsp freshly squeezed
orange juice

4 tbsp
maple syrup

8 large fresh figs,
chopped

6 ice cubes

to decorate

toasted chopped
hazelnuts

✳ Pour the yogurt, orange juice, and maple syrup into a food processor and process gently until combined.

✳ Add the figs and ice cubes and process until smooth. Pour the mixture into glasses and sprinkle over some toasted chopped hazelnuts. Serve at once.

red bell pepper
booster

how hard ✳ extremely easy
serves ✳ two
prep time ✳ 15 minutes
cooking time ✳ —

ingredients

1 cup
carrot juice

1 cup
tomato juice

2 large red bell peppers,
seeded and coarsely chopped

1 tbsp
lemon juice

to serve

freshly ground
black pepper

✳ Pour the carrot juice and tomato juice into a food processor and process gently until combined.

✳ Add the red bell peppers and lemon juice. Season with plenty of freshly ground black pepper and process until smooth. Pour the mixture into tall glasses, add straws, and serve.

ginger
crush

how hard ✳ very easy
serves ✳ two
prep time ✳ 15 minutes
cooking time ✳ —

ingredients

1 cup
carrot juice

4 tomatoes,
skinned, seeded, and
coarsely chopped

1 tbsp
lemon juice

1 oz/25 g
fresh parsley

1 tbsp grated
fresh gingerroot

6 ice cubes

½ cup
water

to garnish

chopped fresh **parsley**

✳ Put the carrot juice, tomatoes, and lemon juice into a food processor and process gently until combined.

✳ Add the parsley to the food processor along with the ginger and ice cubes. Process until well combined, then pour in the water and process until smooth.

✳ Pour the mixture into glasses and garnish with chopped fresh parsley. Serve at once.

cranberry
energizer

how hard ☀ extremely easy

serves ☀ two

prep time ☀ 10 minutes

cooking time ☀ —

ingredients

1¼ cups
cranberry juice

scant ½ cup
orange juice

5½ oz/150 g
fresh raspberries

1 tbsp
lemon juice

to decorate

slices and spirals
of fresh **lemon**
or **orange**

✳ Pour the cranberry juice and orange juice into a food processor and process gently until combined. Add the raspberries and lemon juice and process until smooth.

✳ Pour the mixture into glasses and decorate with slices and spirals of fresh lemon or orange. Serve at once.

nectarine
melt

how hard ✳ extremely easy
serves ✳ two
prep time ✳ 15 minutes
cooking time ✳ —

ingredients

1 cup
milk

12 oz/350 g
lemon sherbet

1 ripe mango,
pitted and diced

2 ripe nectarines,
pitted and diced

✳ Pour the milk into a food processor, add half of the lemon sherbet, and process until combined. Add the remaining sherbet and process until smooth.

✳ When the mixture is thoroughly blended, gradually add the mango and nectarines and process until smooth. Pour the mixture into glasses, add straws, and serve.

peppermint
ice

how hard ✳ extremely easy
serves ✳ two
prep time ✳ 10 minutes
cooking time ✳ —

ingredients

⅔ cup
milk

2 tbsp
peppermint syrup

14 oz/400 g
peppermint ice cream

to decorate

sprigs of fresh **mint**

✳ Pour the milk and peppermint syrup into a food processor and process gently until combined.

✳ Add the peppermint ice cream and process until smooth. Pour the mixture into tall glasses and decorate with sprigs of fresh mint. Add straws and serve.

cinnamon & lemon

tea

how hard ✳ extremely easy

serves ✳ two

prep time ✳ 8–10 minutes

cooking time ✳ 3–4 minutes

ingredients

1¾ cups
water

4 cloves

1 small stick of
cinnamon

2 tea bags

3–4 tbsp
lemon juice

1–2 tbsp
brown sugar

to decorate

slices of fresh **lemon**

✳ Put the water, cloves, and cinnamon stick into a pan and bring to a boil. Remove from the heat and add the tea bags. Let stand for 5 minutes to infuse, then remove the tea bags.

✳ Stir in lemon juice and sugar to taste. Return the pan to the heat and warm through gently.

✳ Remove the pan from the heat and strain the tea into heatproof glasses. Decorate with slices of fresh lemon and serve.

orange & lime iced

tea

how hard ✳ very easy

serves ✳ two

prep time ✳ 15 minutes
+ 1¼ hours to chill

cooking time ✳ 3–4 minutes

ingredients

1¼ cups
water

2 tea bags

scant ½ cup
orange juice

4 tbsp
lime juice

1–2 tbsp
brown sugar

8 ice cubes

to decorate

wedge of **lime**

granulated **sugar**

slices of fresh **orange,
lemon,** or **lime**

✳ Pour the water into a pan and bring to a boil. Remove from the heat, add the tea bags, and let stand for 5 minutes to infuse. Remove the tea bags and let the tea cool to room temperature (about 30 minutes). Transfer to a pitcher, cover with plastic wrap, and chill in the refrigerator for at least 45 minutes.

✳ When the tea has chilled, pour in the orange juice and lime juice. Add sugar to taste.

✳ Take two glasses and rub the rims with a wedge of lime, then dip them in granulated sugar to frost. Put the ice cubes into the glasses and pour over the tea. Decorate the rims with slices of fresh orange, lemon, or lime and serve.

healthy lunches

Make your lunches special with the delightful drinks on the following pages. They are packed with life-giving nutrients and use the freshest, most delicious ingredients. Why not try the Watercress Float, which is rich in vitamin A and iron, or the Celery Surprise, a fortifying tonic for mind and body? If a dessert drink is more to your taste, the Berry Cream is a satisfying way to finish your meal, and the Banana & Blueberry Smoothie will add some sparkle to your midday break.

berry

cream

how hard ✳ extremely easy

serves ✳ two

prep time ✳ 10 minutes

cooking time ✳ —

ingredients

1½ cups
orange juice

1 banana,
sliced and frozen

1 lb/450 g frozen
forest fruits
(such as blueberries,
raspberries,
and blackberries)

to decorate

slices of fresh
strawberry

✳ Pour the orange juice into a food processor. Add the banana and half of the forest fruits and process until smooth.

✳ Add the remaining forest fruits and process until smooth. Pour the mixture into tall glasses and decorate the rims with slices of fresh strawberry. Add straws and serve.

banana & blueberry
smoothie

how hard ✳ extremely easy
serves ✳ two
prep time ✳ 10 minutes
cooking time ✳ —

ingredients

¾ cup
apple juice
½ cup
plain yogurt
1 banana,
sliced and frozen
6 oz/175 g frozen
blueberries

to decorate

whole fresh
blueberries

✳ Pour the apple juice into a food processor. Add the yogurt and process until smooth.

✳ Add the banana and half of the blueberries and process well, then add the remaining blueberries and process until smooth. Pour the mixture into tall glasses and decorate with whole fresh blueberries. Add straws and serve.

banana & apple
booster

how hard ❊ extremely easy

serves ❊ two

prep time ❊ 15 minutes

cooking time ❊ —

ingredients

1 cup
apple juice

½ tsp powdered
cinnamon

2 tsp grated
fresh gingerroot

2 bananas,
sliced and frozen

to decorate

slices of fresh
banana
on toothpicks

❊ Pour the apple juice into a food processor. Add the cinnamon and ginger and process gently until combined.

❊ Add the bananas and process until smooth. Pour the mixture into tall glasses and decorate with slices of fresh banana on toothpicks. Add straws and serve.

strawberry & orange
smoothie

how hard ☀ extremely easy
serves ☀ two
prep time ☀ 15 minutes
cooking time ☀ —

ingredients

½ cup
plain yogurt

¾ cup
strawberry yogurt

¾ cup
orange juice

6 oz/175 g frozen
strawberries

1 banana,
sliced and frozen

to decorate

slices of fresh **orange**

whole fresh
strawberries

✳ Pour the plain and strawberry yogurts into a food processor and process gently. Add the orange juice and process the mix until well combined.

✳ Add the strawberries and banana and process until smooth. Pour the mixture into tall glasses and decorate with slices of fresh orange and whole fresh strawberries. Add straws and serve.

celery

surprise

how hard ✳ very easy
serves ✳ two
prep time ✳ 15 minutes
cooking time ✳ —

ingredients

½ cup
carrot juice

1 lb 2 oz/500 g
tomatoes,
skinned, seeded, and
coarsely chopped

1 tbsp
lemon juice

4 celery stalks,
trimmed and sliced

4 scallions,
trimmed and coarsely chopped

1 oz/25 g
fresh parsley

1 oz/25 g
fresh mint

to garnish

2 **celery** stalks

✳ Put the carrot juice, tomatoes, and lemon juice into a food processor and process gently until combined.

✳ Add the sliced celery along with the scallions, parsley, and mint, and process until smooth. Pour the mixture into tall glasses and garnish with celery stalks. Serve at once.

curried
crush

how hard ✳ very easy
serves ✳ two
prep time ✳ 15 minutes
cooking time ✳ —

ingredients

1 cup
carrot juice
4 tomatoes,
skinned, seeded, and
coarsely chopped
1 tbsp
lemon juice
2 celery stalks,
trimmed and sliced
1 Romaine lettuce
1 garlic clove,
chopped
1 oz/25 g
fresh parsley
1 tsp
curry powder
6 ice cubes
½ cup
water

to garnish
2 celery stalks

✳ Put the carrot juice, tomatoes, lemon juice, and celery into a food processor and process gently until combined.

✳ Separate the lettuce leaves, then wash them and add them to the food processor along with the garlic, parsley, curry powder, and ice cubes. Process until well combined, then pour in the water and process until smooth.

✳ Pour the mixture into tall glasses and garnish with celery stalks. Serve at once.

watercress
float

how hard ✳ extremely easy
serves ✳ two
prep time ✳ 10 minutes
+ 1 hour to chill
cooking time ✳ —

ingredients

generous 2 cups
carrot juice

1 oz/25 g
watercress or arugula

1 tbsp
lemon juice

to garnish

sprigs of fresh
watercress, arugula,
or baby **spinach**

✳ Pour the carrot juice into a food processor. Add the watercress or arugula and the lemon juice and process until smooth. Transfer to a pitcher, cover with plastic wrap, and chill in the refrigerator for at least 1 hour, or until required.

✳ When the mixture is thoroughly chilled, pour into glasses and garnish with sprigs of fresh watercress, arugula, or baby spinach. Serve at once.

summer & citrus fruit
punch

how hard ✳ extremely easy
serves ✳ two
prep time ✳ 10 minutes
cooking time ✳ —

ingredients

4 tbsp
orange juice

1 tbsp
lime juice

scant ½ cup
sparkling water

12 oz/350 g frozen
summer fruits
(such as blueberries, raspberries,
blackberries, and strawberries)

4 ice cubes

to decorate

whole fresh
**raspberries,
blackcurrants,**
and **blackberries**
on toothpicks

✳ Pour the orange juice, lime juice, and sparkling water into a food processor and process gently until combined.

✳ Add the summer fruits and ice cubes and process until a slushy consistency has been reached.

✳ Pour the mixture into glasses, decorate with whole raspberries, blackcurrants, and blackberries on toothpicks, and serve.

strawberry & peach smoothie

how hard ✲ very easy
serves ✲ two
prep time ✲ 20 minutes
cooking time ✲ —

ingredients

3/4 cup **milk**

8 oz/225 g canned **peach slices,** drained

2 fresh apricots, chopped

14 oz/400 g **fresh strawberries,** hulled and sliced

2 bananas, sliced and frozen

to decorate

slices of fresh **strawberries**

* Pour the milk into a food processor. Add the peach slices and process gently until combined. Add the apricots and process gently until combined.

* Add the strawberries and banana slices and process until smooth. Pour the mixture into glasses and decorate the rims with slices of fresh strawberries. Serve at once.

fruit
rapture

how hard ❇ extremely easy
serves ❇ two
prep time ❇ 15 minutes
cooking time ❇ —

ingredients

scant ½ cup
milk

½ cup
peach yogurt

6 tbsp
orange juice

8 oz/225 g canned
peach slices,
drained

6 ice cubes

to decorate

fresh strips of
orange peel

❇ Pour the milk, yogurt, and orange juice into a food processor and process gently until combined.

❇ Add the peach slices and ice cubes and process until smooth. Pour the mixture into glasses and decorate with strips of orange peel. Add straws and serve.

homemade
lemonade

how hard ✳ very easy
serves ✳ two
prep time ✳ 15 minutes
+ 2½ hours to chill
cooking time ✳ 8–10 minutes

ingredients

²/₃ cup
water

6 tbsp
sugar

1 tsp grated
lemon zest

½ cup
lemon juice

6 ice cubes

to decorate

wedge of **lemon**
granulated **sugar**
slices of fresh **lemon**

to serve

sparkling **water**

✳ Put the water, sugar, and lemon zest into a small pan and bring to a boil, stirring constantly. Continue to boil, stirring, for 5 minutes.

✳ Remove from the heat and let cool to room temperature. Stir in the lemon juice, then transfer to a pitcher, cover with plastic wrap, and chill in the refrigerator for at least 2 hours.

✳ When the lemon mixture has almost finished chilling, take two glasses and rub the rims with a wedge of lemon, then dip them in granulated sugar to frost. Put the ice cubes into the glasses.

✳ Remove the lemon mixture from the refrigerator, pour it over the ice, and top up with sparkling water. The ratio should be one part lemon mixture to three parts sparkling water. Stir well to mix, decorate with slices of fresh lemon, and serve.

dinner desserts

You are in for a real treat with these dinner drinks, which are guaranteed to delight your family and friends. The Rich Chocolate Shake will enchant the chocolate lovers among you, and the Kiwi Dream will provide a refreshing and flavorsome finale to your meal. If you would like to add a twist to the after-dinner coffee theme, the Hazelnut & Coffee Sparkle will be a talking point, and the Pineapple Soda is a stunning drink to serve outside on warm evenings.

spicy banana
chill

how hard ❊ extremely easy
serves ❊ two
prep time ❊ 10 minutes
cooking time ❊ —

ingredients

1¼ cups
milk

½ tsp
allspice

5½ oz/150 g
banana ice cream

2 bananas,
sliced and frozen

❊ Pour the milk into a food processor and add the allspice. Add half of the banana ice cream and process gently until combined, then add the remaining ice cream and process until well blended.

❊ When the mixture is well combined, add the bananas and process until smooth. Pour the mixture into tall glasses, add straws, and serve at once.

banana & coffee
milkshake

how hard ❊ extremely easy
serves ❊ two
prep time ❊ 10 minutes
cooking time ❊ —

ingredients

1¼ cups
milk

4 tbsp
instant coffee powder

5½ oz/150 g
vanilla ice cream

2 bananas,
sliced and frozen

✳ Pour the milk into a food processor, add the coffee powder, and process gently until combined. Add half of the vanilla ice cream and process gently, then add the remaining ice cream and process until well combined.

✳ When the mixture is thoroughly blended, add the bananas and process until smooth. Pour the mixture into glasses and serve.

rich chocolate
shake

how hard ✳ extremely easy

serves ✳ two

prep time ✳ 10 minutes

cooking time ✳ —

ingredients

²⁄₃ cup
milk

2 tbsp
chocolate syrup

14 oz/400 g
chocolate ice cream

to decorate
grated **chocolate**

✳ Pour the milk and chocolate syrup into a food processor and process gently until combined.

✳ Add the chocolate ice cream and process until smooth. Pour the mixture into tall glasses and decorate by floating the grated chocolate. Serve at once.

maple & almond
milkshake

how hard ❊ extremely easy
serves ❊ two
prep time ❊ 15 minutes
cooking time ❊ —

ingredients

²/₃ cup
milk

2 tbsp
maple syrup

14 oz/400 g
vanilla ice cream

1 tbsp
almond extract

to decorate

chopped **almonds**

❊ Pour the milk and maple syrup into a food processor and process gently until combined.

❊ Add the ice cream and almond extract and process until smooth. Pour the mixture into glasses and decorate with the chopped almonds. Add straws and serve.

kiwi
dream

how hard ✳ extremely easy
serves ✳ two
prep time ✳ 15 minutes
cooking time ✳ —

ingredients

²/₃ cup
milk

juice of
2 limes

2 kiwifruit,
chopped

1 tbsp
sugar

14 oz/400 g
vanilla ice cream

to decorate

slices of fresh
kiwifruit

strips of fresh
lime peel

✳ Pour the milk and lime juice into a food processor and process gently until combined.

✳ Add the chopped kiwis and sugar and process gently, then add the ice cream and process until smooth. Pour the mixture into glasses and decorate with slices of fresh kiwifruit and strips of fresh lime peel. Serve at once.

coffee
whip

how hard ✻ extremely easy

serves ✻ two

prep time ✻ 15 minutes

cooking time ✻ —

ingredients

generous ¾ cup
milk

scant ¼ cup
light cream

1 tbsp
brown sugar

2 tbsp
unsweetened cocoa

1 tbsp
coffee syrup
or instant coffee powder

6 ice cubes

to serve

whipped **cream**

grated **chocolate**

✳ Put the milk, cream, and sugar into a food processor, and process gently until combined.

✳ Add the unsweetened cocoa and coffee syrup or powder and process well, then add the ice cubes and process until smooth.

✳ Pour the mixture into glasses. Top with whipped cream, sprinkle over the grated chocolate, and serve.

smooth iced
coffee

how hard ❉ very easy
serves ❉ two
prep time ❉ 15 minutes
+ 1¼ hours to chill
cooking time ❉ —

ingredients

1³/₄ cups
water

2 tbsp
instant coffee powder

2 tbsp
brown sugar
6 ice cubes

to decorate

light **cream**
whole **coffee** beans

❉ Use the water and coffee powder to brew some hot coffee, then let cool to room temperature. Transfer to a pitcher, cover with plastic wrap, and chill in the refrigerator for at least 45 minutes.

❉ When the coffee has chilled, pour it into a food processor. Add the sugar, and process until well combined. Add the ice cubes and process until smooth.

❉ Pour the mixture into glasses. Float light cream on top, decorate with whole coffee beans, and serve.

hazelnut & coffee
sparkle

how hard ✳ extremely easy
serves ✳ two
prep time ✳ 15 minutes
+ 1¼ hours to chill
cooking time ✳ —

ingredients

1 cup
water

3 tbsp
instant coffee powder

½ cup
sparkling water

1 tbsp
hazelnut syrup

2 tbsp
brown sugar
6 ice cubes

to decorate

slices of fresh
lime

slices of fresh
lemon

✳ Use the water and coffee powder to brew some hot coffee, then let cool to room temperature. Transfer to a pitcher, cover with plastic wrap, and chill in the refrigerator for at least 45 minutes.

✳ When the coffee has chilled, pour it into a food processor. Add the sparkling water, hazelnut syrup, and sugar, and process well. Add the ice cubes and process until smooth.

✳ Pour the mixture into glasses, decorate the rims with slices of fresh lime and lemon, and serve.

pineapple
soda

how hard ✳ easy
serves ✳ two
prep time ✳ 15–20 minutes
cooking time ✳ —

ingredients

¾ cup
pineapple juice

⅓ cup
coconut milk

7 oz/200 g
vanilla ice cream

5 oz/140 g frozen
pineapple chunks

¾ cup
sparkling water

to serve

2 scooped-out
pineapple shells
(optional)

✳ Pour the pineapple juice and coconut milk into a food processor. Add the ice cream and process until smooth.

✳ Add the pineapple chunks and process well. Pour the mixture into scooped-out pineapple shells or tall glasses, until two-thirds full. Top up with sparkling water, add straws, and serve.

orange & carrot

smoothie

how hard ✳ extremely easy

serves ✳ two

prep time ✳ 10 minutes

cooking time ✳ —

ingredients

¾ cup
carrot juice

¾ cup
orange juice

5½ oz/150 g
vanilla ice cream

6 ice cubes

decoration

slices of fresh
orange

strips of fresh
orange peel

✳ Pour the carrot juice and orange juice into a food processor and process gently until well combined. Add the ice cream and process until thoroughly blended.

✳ Add the ice cubes and process until smooth. Pour the mixture into glasses, decorate with slices of fresh orange and strips of fresh orange peel, and serve.

evening cocktails

How could we finish this book without a tempting selection of cocktails? This section contains some truly mouthwatering concoctions, which are perfect for entertaining or when you have a few relaxing moments to yourself. When hosting a party, serve your guests the spectacular looking Pineapple & Coconut Shake. For more intimate moments, the Cherry Kiss will bring a touch of romance to any occasion, and the Rose Sunset will prove irresistible as the sun goes down.

pineapple & coconut
shake

how hard ✳ very easy
serves ✳ two
prep time ✳ 15 minutes
cooking time ✳ —

ingredients

1½ cups
pineapple juice

⅓ cup
coconut milk

5½ oz/150 g
vanilla ice cream

5 oz/140 g frozen
pineapple chunks

to serve

2 scooped-out
coconut shells
(optional)

to decorate

2 tbsp grated fresh
coconut

✳ Pour the pineapple juice and coconut milk into a food processor. Add the ice cream and process until smooth.

✳ Add the pineapple chunks and process until smooth. Pour the mixture into scooped-out coconut shells, or tall glasses, and decorate with grated fresh coconut. Add straws and serve.

peach & pineapple
smoothie

how hard ✳ extremely easy

serves ✳ two

prep time ✳ 15 minutes

cooking time ✳ —

ingredients

½ cup
pineapple juice

juice of
1 lemon

scant ½ cup
water

3 tbsp
brown sugar

¾ cup
plain yogurt

1 peach,
cut into chunks and frozen

3½ oz/100 g frozen
pineapple chunks

to decorate

wedges of fresh
pineapple

✳ Pour the pineapple juice, lemon juice, and water into a food processor. Add the sugar and yogurt and process until blended.

✳ Add the peach and pineapple chunks and process until smooth. Pour the mixture into glasses and decorate the rims with wedges of fresh pineapple. Serve at once.

caribbean vegan
cocktail

ingredients

scant ½ cup
coconut milk

generous ¾ cup
soy milk

6 tbsp
pineapple juice

1 tbsp
brown sugar

1 ripe mango,
pitted and diced

2 tbsp grated
fresh coconut

5 oz/140 g frozen
pineapple chunks

1 banana,
sliced and frozen

to decorate
grated fresh **coconut**
wedges of fresh
pineapple

✳ Put the coconut milk, soy milk, pineapple juice, and sugar into a food processor and process gently until combined. Add the diced mango to the food processor along with the grated coconut and process well.

✳ Add the pineapple chunks and banana and process until smooth. Pour the mixture into glasses, sprinkle over some grated fresh coconut, and decorate the rims with wedges of fresh pineapple. Serve at once.

red
storm

how hard ❊ extremely easy
serves ❊ two
prep time ❊ 15 minutes
+ 30 minutes to chill
cooking time ❊ —

ingredients

generous 2 cups
tomato juice
dash of
Worcestershire sauce
1 small red chile,
seeded and chopped
1 scallion,
trimmed and chopped
6 ice cubes

to garnish
2 long, thin red **chiles,**
cut into flowers (see method)

❊ To make the chile flowers, use a sharp knife to make six cuts along each chile. Place the point of the knife about ½ inch/1 cm from the stem end and cut toward the tip. Put the chiles in a bowl of iced water and let stand for about 25–30 minutes, until they have spread out into flower shapes.

❊ Put the tomato juice and Worcestershire sauce into a food processor and process gently until combined. Add the chopped chile, scallion, and ice cubes, and process until smooth.

❊ Pour the mixture into glasses and garnish with the chile flowers. Add straws and serve.

peppermint
mocha

how hard ✳ extremely easy
serves ✳ two
prep time ✳ 15 minutes
cooking time ✳ —

ingredients

1³/₄ cups
milk

generous ³/₄ cup
coffee syrup

scant ½ cup
peppermint syrup

1 tbsp chopped
fresh mint leaves

4 ice cubes

to decorate

grated **chocolate**

sprigs of fresh **mint**

✳ Pour the milk, coffee syrup, and peppermint syrup into a food processor and process gently until combined.

✳ Add the mint and ice cubes and process until a slushy consistency has been reached.

✳ Pour the mixture into glasses. Sprinkle over the grated chocolate, decorate with sprigs of fresh mint, and serve.

pineapple
crush

how hard ❄ extremely easy
serves ❄ two
prep time ❄ 10 minutes
cooking time ❄ —

ingredients

scant ½ cup
pineapple juice

4 tbsp
orange juice

4½ oz/125 g
galia melon,
cut into chunks

5 oz/140 g frozen
pineapple chunks

4 ice cubes

to decorate
slices of galia melon
slices of orange

❋ Pour the pineapple juice and orange juice into a food processor and process gently until combined.

❋ Add the melon, pineapple chunks, and ice cubes, and process until a slushy consistency has been reached.

❋ Pour the mixture into glasses and decorate with slices of melon and orange. Serve at once.

hawaiian
shake

how hard ✳ very easy
serves ✳ two
prep time ✳ 15 minutes
cooking time ✳ —

ingredients

1 cup
milk

scant ¼ cup
coconut milk

5½ oz/150 g
vanilla ice cream

2 bananas,
sliced and frozen

7 oz/200 g canned
pineapple chunks,
drained

1 papaya,
seeded and diced

to decorate

grated fresh
coconut

wedges of fresh
pineapple

✳ Pour the milk and coconut milk into a food processor and process gently until combined. Add half of the ice cream and process gently, then add the remaining ice cream and process until smooth.

✳ Add the bananas and process well, then add the pineapple chunks and papaya and process until smooth. Pour the mixture into tall glasses, sprinkle over the grated coconut, and decorate the rims with wedges of fresh pineapple. Serve at once.

rose

sunset

how hard ✳ very easy
serves ✳ two
prep time ✳ 15 minutes
cooking time ✳ —

ingredients

scant ½ cup
plain yogurt

generous 2 cups
milk

1 tbsp
rose water

3 tbsp
honey

1 ripe mango,
pitted and diced

6 ice cubes

to decorate

edible **rose petals**
(optional)

✳ Pour the yogurt and milk into a food processor and process gently until combined.

✳ Add the rose water and honey and process until thoroughly blended, then add the mango along with the ice cubes and process until smooth. Pour the mixture into glasses, decorate with edible rose petals, if using, and serve.

cherry
kiss

how hard ✳ extremely easy

serves ✳ two

prep time ✳ 5 minutes

cooking time ✳ —

ingredients

8 ice cubes,
crushed

2 tbsp
cherry syrup

generous 2 cups
sparkling water

to decorate
maraschino cherries
on toothpicks

✳ Divide the crushed ice between two tall glasses and pour over the cherry syrup.

✳ Top up each glass with sparkling water. Decorate with the maraschino cherries on toothpicks and serve.

raspberry
cooler

how hard ✳ extremely easy
serves ✳ two
prep time ✳ 5 minutes
cooking time ✳ —

ingredients

8 ice cubes,
crushed

2 tbsp
raspberry syrup

generous 2 cups
chilled apple juice

to decorate

whole fresh
raspberries
and pieces of
apple
on toothpicks

✳ Divide the crushed ice between two glasses and pour over the

raspberry syrup.

✳ Top up each glass with chilled apple juice and stir well.

Decorate with the whole fresh raspberries and pieces of apple on

toothpicks and serve at once.

index